Color in My World

Green Around Me

Oscar Cantillo

Cavendish Square

New York

Published in 2015 by Cavendish Square Publishing, LLC
243 5th Avenue, Suite 136, New York, NY 10016

First Edition

Website: cavendishsq.com

This publication represents the opinions and views of the author based on his or her personal experience, knowledge, and research. The information in this book serves as a general guide only. The author and publisher have used their best efforts in preparing this book and disclaim liability rising directly or indirectly from the use and application of this book.

CPSIA Compliance Information: Batch #WW15CSQ

All websites were available and accurate when this book was sent to press.

Library of Congress Cataloging-in-Publication Data

Cantillo, Oscar, author.
Green around me / Oscar Cantillo.
pages cm. — (Color in my world)
Includes index.
ISBN 978-1-50260-066-0 (hardcover) ISBN 978-1-50260-276-3 (paperback) ISBN 978-1-50260-068-4 (ebook)
1. Green—Juvenile literature. 2. Colors—Juvenile literature. 3. Color—Juvenile literature. I. Title.
QC495.5.C367 2015
535.6—dc23
2014032622

9903

Editor: Andrew Coddington
Senior Copy Editor: Wendy A. Reynolds
Art Director: Jeffrey Talbot
Designer: Joseph Macri
Senior Production Manager: Jennifer Ryder-Talbot
Production Editor: David McNamara
Photo Researcher: J8 Media

Printed in the United States of America

Contents

Green Everywhere **4**

New Words **22**

Index **23**

About the Author **24**

The color green is everywhere!

Trees have green leaves.

Trees stretch high into the sky.

5

Clovers are green.

They cover fields like a green blanket.

7

Many **vegetables** are green.

You can buy them at a grocery store.

They are very **healthy**!

9

Limes are a green fruit.

They are very **tart** to taste.

This frog is green.

He is hopping from leaf to leaf.

13

Grasshoppers live in green grass.

They are green like their homes.

15

Dollars are green.

We use them to buy things.

This **stoplight** is showing green.

It is saying it is safe to drive.

18

19

It is St. Patrick's Day!

People wear green
to **celebrate**.

21

New Words

celebrate (SEL-a-brayt) To join a fun social activity.

healthy (HEL-thee) Good for you.

stoplight (STAHP-lite) A signal used to control traffic.

tart (TART) Sharp or sour taste.

vegetables (VEJ-teh-bulz) Plants or parts of plants used as food.

22

Index

celebrate, 20

fruit, 10

healthy, 8

stoplight, 18
St. Patrick's Day, 20

tart, 10
taste, 10

vegetables, 8

23

About the Author

Oscar Cantillo is a writer. He lives near the ocean with his partner and two daughters. They all love watching beautiful shades of blue and green in the water.

About BOOKWORMS

Bookworms help independent readers gain reading confidence through high-frequency words, simple sentences, and strong picture/text support. Each book explores a concept that helps children relate what they read to the world they live in.